Little Cat is hungry

Story by Annette Smith
Illustrations by Ben Spiby

Little Cat

Here comes Little Cat.

Little Cat is hungry.

"Meow! Meow! Meow!"

Little Cat can see a lizard.

The lizard is asleep
in the sun.

Here comes Little Cat.

The lizard wakes up.

Look at the lizard.

Little Cat can see a bird.

The bird can not see Little Cat.

Here comes Little Cat.

The bird sees Little Cat.

The bird is up in a big tree.

Little Cat looks up at the bird.

Little Cat is hungry.
"Meow! Meow! Meow!"

"Here you are, Little Cat."